The **Faith in Action** Series

Son of Africa

The Story of Olaudah Equiano and the Campaign Against the Slave Trade

Chris Hudson

Illustrated by Paul Bryn Davies

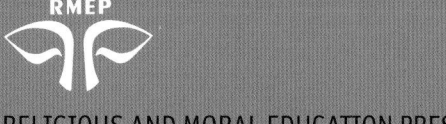

RELIGIOUS AND MORAL EDUCATION PRESS

SON OF AFRICA

The Story of Olaudah Equiano and the Campaign Against the Slave Trade

Imagine a ship, an old wooden ship with tall masts, sailing helplessly through high waves into a raging storm that will shortly tear it to pieces. The sails are in tatters, the masts broken. Nature is about to punish its crew for their crimes. In the ship's wake, you can see bodies floating, human bodies with legs and arms in chains. Some in the water are still alive, their desperate hands stretching, grasping up in horror, with no hope of rescue. And close by, you can see sharks circling, gathering for the feast. The swirling sky and sea are turning red, a deep blood-red. Everything is lost.

You are imagining the scene of a painting created by Joseph Turner in 1840, entitled 'Slave ship'. It is based on a real-life incident in 1781 – but what actually happened was far worse. There was no raging storm, no shipwreck, and the crew survived. The people in the water *were* really thrown overboard to die, but simply to save someone money. It happened like this.

The *Zong* Massacre

'What do you mean, we're lost?' James Kelsall was registered as first mate on the *Zong*, a Liverpool ship carrying 442 Africans to be sold into slavery in Jamaica – only they couldn't find Jamaica.

'That's what the Captain says!' growled another seaman. 'The officers are meeting now.'

'I wonder what they'll decide,' James muttered. It didn't look good. They were nearly out of fresh water and food – and disease had broken out. Having taken on too many slaves to start with (to increase the profits) the *Zong* had already lost sixty enslaved Africans to sickness along with seven of the English crew, their corpses all thrown overboard. Captain Collingwood couldn't navigate to save his own life. (How do you *miss* an island the size of Jamaica?) The crew were called together, and Collingwood stood up nervously to speak.

'I've come to a decision. Owing to sheer bad luck, we're in serious danger of losing the whole cargo and our own lives. There's only one sensible thing to do now – start dumping the sick ones overboard to stop the disease and save water.'

James couldn't believe it. 'The sick ones, sir? While they're still alive?'

Collingwood suddenly glared. 'Are you questioning my judgement, sir?' His tone had changed. Challenging the master and commander of a ship could be a bad move, but James nervously stood his ground.

'No, sir, but … can we afford it? Surely they'll last a few more days, sir.'

The captain smiled. 'We can't afford sickness on board, Mr Kelsall. I need my crew and we all need fresh water. Death of cargo through sickness counts as a natural loss, and we lose money – but dumping cargo to save the ship and crew is covered by insurance. The insurance company may lose money, but you and I won't.'

James fell silent. You couldn't argue with money. Profit was the whole point of the voyage – and the water supplies were low.

And so it was done. One by one, the slaves were brought up out of the stinking hold and inspected. Fit ones were sent back down. The sick, fifty-four in all, were dragged, resisting all the way, to the side of the ship and thrown overboard, men, women and children, young and old – all of them still alive and in chains. Next day, forty-two more suffered the same fate. On the following day (despite a shower of rain that improved the supply of drinking water), it was another twenty-six. In all, 133 people were killed because of Collingwood's decision.

When the ship finally docked in Jamaica (to sell its remaining slaves at a good profit), James made a strange discovery in the ship's stores. The *Zong still* had about 1900 litres of fresh water to spare. He decided to remember this…

What Do You Think?

Important: In answering 'What Do You Think?' questions in this book, it is important that you not only state your opinion but also give as many reasons as possible for your opinion.

1. How do you think Captain Collingwood viewed his slaves?

2. What can happen when people stop seeing other people as human beings, and treat them as objects?

3. How would you have reacted if you had been on the *Zong* and, at the end of the voyage, you had learned that there was so much water left?

Captured

In 1789 a remarkable autobiography was published. In it, a former enslaved African recounted his fight for freedom. Olaudah Equiano said he was born in 1745 at Essaka in the district of Eboe, to the west of what we now call Nigeria. He had a happy childhood growing up in a traditional African village as the son of a chief. It was a place where people grew their own food and kept their own animals. He tells us that, 'Our land is uncommonly rich and fruitful, and produces all kind of vegetables in great abundance.' Everyone worked together in the fields, so everyone had something to do – and there were no beggars. Equiano trained as a farmer and as a warrior, for each village had to be able to protect itself from bandits.

However, Equiano's autobiography tells us that his life changed dramatically when he was 11 years old. One day when his parents were away, he and his sister were abducted from their own home by slave-traders. Two men and a woman crept into the house, covered the children's mouths to prevent their crying out, bound them with cords, then carried them away.

After several days' travel, the children were then sold – like animals. Although some forms of slavery had been common in this part of Africa for hundreds of years this was different.

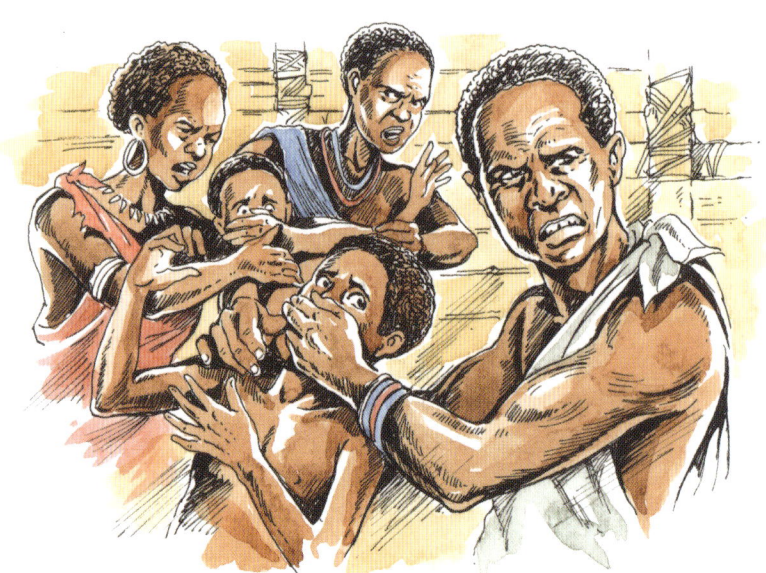

Usually the slaves were treated well, and almost thought of as members of the family. (Their children were free and didn't automatically become slaves themselves.) But as Equiano was passed on from seller to seller, he was taken closer to the Atlantic coast, where the treatment of slaves was more cruel. He saw his sister once more, and then never again: after seven months, he was cut off from everything he knew. Then on one fateful day, they reached the Atlantic coast. Equiano found himself staring at his first view of a slave-ship, and his first 'white men' – then he was taken on board.

Equiano was kept in chains below deck – until the day another vessel came to take him across the ocean. Who were these white men? What creatures were they, with their long hair, their red faces, and strange talk? At first he thought they were cannibals. Did they drink human blood? Was he going to be eaten? Equiano refused to eat, vowing to starve himself to death, but was beaten until he took food again. (The African slave-traders never acted like this!) He once even saw a white man being savagely beaten to death by the ship's captain. What was going on?

Soon, he would be taken across the sea to a new land called 'Barbadoes' to work for these strange people. Like millions of other Africans, Equiano was taking a one-way trip to the worst place in the world – and he was still only 11 years old.

How slavery changed
Before the Europeans arrived in Africa slaves could be taken for a fixed time, as either:
· prisoners of war or
· criminals being punished, or paying a debt

Things changed with the arrival of the Europeans when people began to be traded as commodities. They had no rights, and children born to slaves also became slaves.

What Do You Think?

1. What does it mean to have no rights? What rights do you think slaves did not have? Give examples.

2. What rights do you enjoy? How would you feel if you lost these rights?

The Deadly Triangle

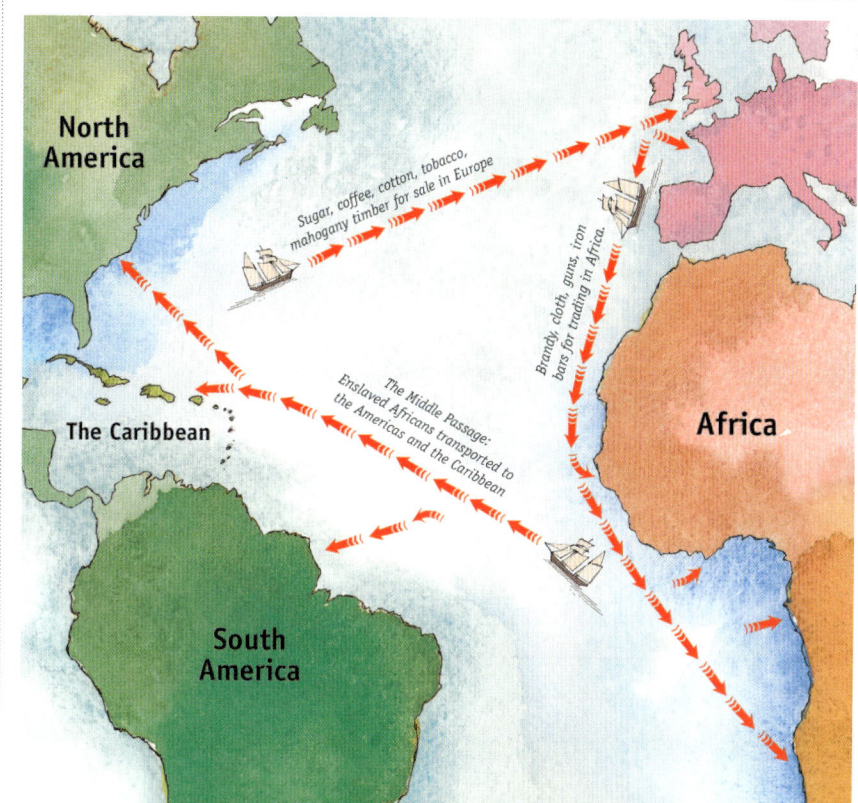

The 'Transatlantic Trade' or 'Middle Passage' was an international money-machine that favoured some people by oppressing a great many others. Slavery had existed in the world since ancient times, but what happened to Equiano was something much bigger, with a greater impact, than anything before: it was the largest forced migration in history.

In 1510, King Ferdinand of Spain had given permission for merchants to take 200 Africans as slaves to the 'New World' (North and South America, and the West Indies) for work in farms, mines and building projects. Africans were selected because they were known to be strong workers who could cope with the heat and hard work on the new plantations, growing sugar, cotton and coffee. They also knew how to raise crops or cattle, and were thought to be 'good-natured', not given to resistance – yet.

Some slaves were captured and taken by Europeans, but the vast majority were actually sold on to Europeans by their fellow Africans on the coast – although the Europeans treated them much more harshly. One traveller said this:

> There is no [European] captain who has carried slaves, who has not been guilty, either directly or indirectly, of murder.

It is now thought that between 9 and 12 million Africans were registered as being shipped across the Atlantic between the years 1492 and 1850. It is unknown how many were transported illegally. All along the Atlantic coast of North and South America, Africans were bought and sold like expensive prize animals to be forced to work in a way unthinkable in Europe, usually in awful conditions. As slavery became outlawed in Europe, it became the norm in America and the West Indies.

The income generated by the slave trade brought incredible wealth to some people and places. There was money to be made in ship-building, marine

Sugar, coffee and other goods produced by slave labour were sold in Europe.

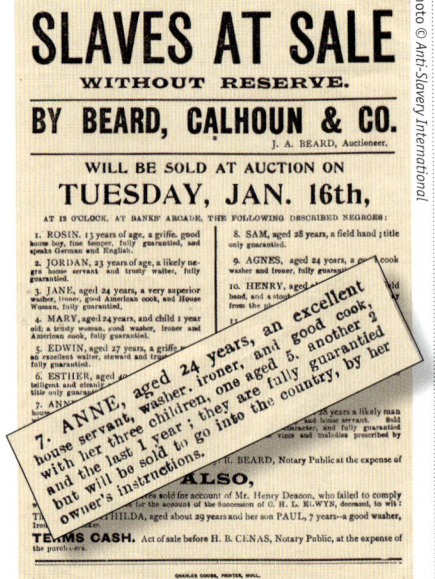

Poster advertising slaves for sale

Ship-building and manufacturing in Europe created wealth and jobs.

insurance, the making of rope, cloth, guns, iron bars, brandy, rum, glass beads, and the refining of sugar.

European goods were traded in Africa for slaves (the most popular products were rolls of cotton and woollen cloth). The enslaved Africans were *then* taken to be sold in America, in exchange for goods that could *then* be sold back in Europe.

In Britain, ports like Bristol and Liverpool grew rich on the proceeds, building themselves brand-new roads, civic buildings and churches. Fortunes made in America were invested in financial centres such as the City of London. Cities like Birmingham prospered from manufacturing products such as guns and bullets, that were then traded in Africa to buy more slaves. Many British cities were involved in some way. Slavery was making Britain 'Great'.

The Trade also made some coastal African rulers more powerful – wars were deliberately fought, some to take slaves from other kingdoms, generating greater wealth for the victors, and others to resist the taking of slaves. However, European influence gradually turned most of these African kingdoms into colonies ruled or 'protected' by European countries. This trend began to be reversed in the 20th century after the Second World War, as many African countries won back their independence – but the effects of the Trade still live on.

Slave-trading ports grew rich.

What Do You Think?

1. In what ways do you think the effects of the slave trade still live on?

Life on Board

What was it like to be on a slave-ship? Equiano described it like this.

'The stench of the hold while we were on the coast was so intolerably loathsome, that it was dangerous to remain there for any time ... some of us [were] permitted to stay on deck for the fresh air: but now that the whole ship's cargo were confined together, it became absolutely pestilential.

'The closeness of the place, and the heat of the climate, added to the number in the ship ... almost suffocated us. This produced copious perspirations, so that the air soon became unfit for respiration, from a variety of loathsome smells, and brought on a sickness among the slaves, of which many died, thus falling victims to the [foolish greed] ... of their purchasers.

'This wretched situation was again aggravated by the galling of the chains, ... and the filth of the necessary tubs, into which the children often fell, and were almost suffocated. The shrieks of the women, and the groans of the dying, rendered the whole a scene of horror almost inconceivable.'

Many didn't survive. John Newton had been a slave-ship captain before his Christian faith led to him becoming an 'Abolitionist'. On joining the campaign against the Trade, he described slave-ship life from personal knowledge:

'[A slave-ship captain will] try to take as many as possible. The cargo of a vessel of a hundred tons [can hold from] two hundred and twenty, to two hundred and fifty slaves. Their lodging-rooms below the deck, which are three [for the men, the boys and the women] besides a place for the sick, are sometimes more than five feet high, and sometimes less; and this height is divided towards the middle, for the slaves lie in two rows, one above the other, on each side of the ship, close to each other, like books upon a shelf. I have known them so close, that the shelf would not easily contain one more …

'… The poor creatures, thus cramped for want of room, are likewise in irons, for the most part both hands and feet, and two together, which makes it difficult for them to turn or move, to attempt either to rise or to lie down, without hurting themselves, or each other … The heat and smell of these rooms, … added to the galling of their irons, and the [depression] which seizes their spirits … soon becomes fatal …

Diagram of the cramped conditions inside a slave-ship

abolitionist: a person who works to bring something to an end, e.g., the end of the slave trade

'[Diseases] often break out, infect[ing] the seamen likewise, and the Oppressors, and the Oppressed, fall by the same stroke. I believe, nearly one half of the slaves on board have sometimes died; and that … the annual loss of life [for all the voyages taken in a given year] cannot be much less than fifteen thousand …'

Inside Knowledge
John Newton's specialist knowledge of the Trade provided the campaigner Thomas Clarkson with crucial evidence about the cruelty suffered both by enslaved Africans and the British crews – all of which was presented in petitions to Parliament. Newton was later ordained as a Christian minister and encouraged William Wilberforce MP to lead the parliamentary campaign against slavery. He also became an author, famous for writing the hymn 'Amazing Grace'.

Another eyewitness, Ottobah Cugoano, taken as a slave from Ghana, remembered this from his experiences.

'It was a most horrible scene; there was nothing to be heard but the rattling of chains, smacking of whips, and the groans and cries of our fellow-men. Some would not stir from the ground when they were lashed and beaten in the most horrible manner ... and when we found ourselves at last taken away, death was more preferable than life ... a plan was concerted amongst us, that we might burn and blow up the ship, and to perish all together in the flames; but we were betrayed ... thousands more have suffered in similar and grievous distress, under the hands of barbarous robbers, and merciless task-masters ...'

Challenging the Trade

How do you stand up and challenge something that everyone around you believes?

From the middle of the 17th century, the slave trade was assumed by almost everyone in Britain to be a necessary engine powering the economy: challenging this would label you as being either mad, bad, or dangerous to know.

But that is exactly what a group of like-minded professionals chose to do from 1792. Labelled the 'Clapham Sect', this informal group of evangelical Christian politicians, civil servants and others began meeting at a house in the village of Clapham, South London, to encourage each other in their faith – and to think seriously about social issues. Pretty quickly they realised that slavery was wrong and that their primary aim had to be the abolition of the slave trade, and so they began to campaign against it.

The names of members such as William Wilberforce, Granville Sharp and Zachary Macaulay would later become household words, as the group used their influence to create a change in public opinion and put pressure on the government. They issued a journal, wrote letters, created petitions, distributed pamphlets, and spoke at public meetings on a range of issues – but abolishing slavery was always their top priority. In time, this group would be a powerful influence – but not yet.

Cugoano was taken and sold on the island of Grenada, then brought to England, where he gained his freedom in 1772. He was baptised into the Christian faith and changed his name to John Stuart. In 1787, he published his autobiography and joined the campaign to abolish slavery.

Despite all these horrors, many slaves found the voyage preferable to what came next.

Photo courtesy Holy Trinity Church, Clapham

Plaque at Holy Trinity Church, Clapham

What Do You Think?

1. How might the traveller have justified accusing all European captains of slave-ships of being guilty of murder (see page 6)? How might the captains have defended themselves? Do you agree with the accusation? Give reasons.

2. Why do you think so many people in Britain supported or accepted the existence of the slave trade?

Life as a Slave

On the Caribbean island of Barbados, Equiano saw friends and families separated and sold in the local slave market. As he watched them taken away in tears, he thought of his own family, an ocean away. Where were they now? Where would *he* be going next?

In fact, Equiano wasn't sold, but shipped to the colony of Virginia and put to work *there* instead. Everything was strange and new. (He had never even seen a horse before.) No-one could speak his language, so he felt isolated and lonely, surrounded by such mysteries as mechanical clocks, which he thought were some kind of demon – because the white men seemed to be obeying them all the time. At one point, he had the job of fanning a sick white gentleman in his bed. When he heard a woman slave arriving to cook the man's dinner, Equiano turned, then gasped in horror. She was wearing a bizarre steel helmet fastened over her head to stop her speaking, eating or drinking – as a punishment, apparently. How could people be so *cruel?*

In time, Equiano was sold as a servant to Michael Pascal, an officer in the British Royal Navy, for forty pounds – and sent to England. (This was his first experience of shipboard life as a passenger instead of being simply 'cargo'.) He was also given a new name, Gustavus Vassa, and beaten when he refused to answer to it. However, he discovered something rather strange about life on board a well-run ship – that if you're useful and reliable, then you become a valuable member of the crew. As he performed jobs around the ship (and did them well), he found that crew-members stopped judging him by the colour of his skin or his slave-status, but instead treated him more like a human being. For the first time since being dragged aboard that slave-ship, Equiano felt his life might just, possibly, be worth living again.

He was now twelve years old. During the voyage, he became firm friends with a lad five years older – a white American named Richard Baker, whose parents were friends of Michael Pascal. Richard became Equiano's companion, guide and teacher of all things new. When they arrived at the port of Falmouth on England's south coast, Equiano was puzzled at the cold white fluffy substance that coated the deck one morning. Was it ... salt? He tasted it – but there was no taste. 'Snow!' he was told. Where did it come from? 'The man in the heavens!' was the reply. Once on land, he was taken to church, and found people worshipping 'God, who made us and all things.' Richard explained things as best he could to Equiano, who remained puzzled – why was it that only Africans were sold in the slave trade and not white people?

Lieutenant Pascal was then given a commission to serve on a series of fighting ships ('men-of-war') – so, naturally, Equiano had to accompany him on his voyages as a personal servant. Despite being enslaved, the boy was now a member of the Royal Navy, and thoroughly enjoying it. He learned how to follow orders, do basic arithmetic, perform men's hairdressing and shaving, tie ropes, haul sails, manage boats, fire a cannon using gunpowder and shot without blowing himself up – and took part in several full-scale sea battles as part of the Seven Years War against the French. Luckily (and unusually), he escaped unhurt.

At one point in a battle, he found himself having to haul a lethal load of gunpowder the whole length of a ship's deck towards some cannon whilst being shot at by the enemy. 'There's a time for me to die as well as to be born,' he thought – but he wasn't going to die *yet*.

In a curious way, despite being enslaved, Equiano felt almost English – he wanted to be more like these new 'countrymen'. He could now speak their language, and wanted to imitate these strange people who seemed to be the lords and masters of the earth. He wanted to 'imbibe their spirit', learn their manners, read and write – and, most especially, he wanted to be baptised as a Christian. It was all a way of 'improving' himself out of slavery, he thought. In 1759, he was baptised at St Margaret's Church in Westminster.

Seven Years War (1756–1763): fighting between the French and the British, but with other European countries becoming involved, over control of Northern America

Others who escaped from slavery had very different stories to tell. Mary Prince was born into slavery on the island of Bermuda in 1788. Both her parents were slaves, so she was born as the property of their owner, hired out to work elsewhere at the age of 12, and then sold along with her mother and her sisters. She recalled it like this:

'At length the [auctioneer], who was to offer us for sale like sheep or cattle, arrived, and asked my mother which was the eldest. She said nothing, but pointed to me. He took me by the hand, and led me out into the middle of the street, and turning me slowly round, exposed me to the view of those who attended the [auction]. I was surrounded by strange men, who examined and handled me in the same manner that a butcher would a calf or a lamb he was about to purchase, and who talked about my shape and size... as if I could no more understand [the] meaning [of the words] than the dumb beasts. I was then put up to sale. The bidding commenced at a few pounds, and gradually rose to fifty-seven. I then saw my sisters led forth, and sold to different owners.'

Mary was taken by her new owners, and remembered this from the following day:

'The next morning my mistress set about instructing me in my tasks. She taught me to do all sorts of household work; to wash and bake, pick cotton and wool, and wash floors, and cook. And she taught me (how can I ever forget it!) more things than these; she taught me to know the exact difference between the smart of the rope, the cart-whip, and the cow-skin, when applied to my naked body by her own cruel hand. And there was scarcely any punishment more dreadful than the blows I received on my face and head from her hard heavy fist. She was a fearful woman, and a savage mistress to her slaves.'

Mary was sold on again to other owners, gradually becoming sick, both from the injuries she received in punishment, and the sheer hard work from dawn to dusk – but she also began attending meetings at a local church where she learned to read and write. In 1828 she was taken to England by her owners, but then escaped, finding refuge with some Christian anti-slavery campaigners. In 1831, she published her autobiography *The History of Mary Prince, A West Indian Slave*, which detailed the abuses she suffered. Her previous owner tried to sue her in court, saying that Mary had 'endeavoured to injure the character of my family by the most vile and infamous falsehoods'. He lost.

What Do You Think?

1. Once in the Navy, Equiano found he was respected and people forgot he was still enslaved. Under what types of circumstances may differences be forgotten?

2. Why do you think Equiano wanted to be like English people? Is imitating someone a good way to become accepted? Why?/Why not?

3. Think about your name. How would you feel if someone changed it to something different? Ottobah Cugoano changed his name to John Stuart (see page 9). Why do you think he did this? Are our names important? Why?/Why not?

A New Master

Equiano thought his good service to Pascal in the Navy would earn him freedom when they arrived back in London, but he was wrong. Despite being baptised, and giving his master all his Royal Navy wages and 'prize-money', Equiano was passed on to a Captain Doran who said 'I talked too much English, and [that] if I did not behave myself well, and be quiet, [then] he had a method on board to make me'. Everything Equiano had saved or bought for himself, even his coat, was taken away from him. It was a 'new slavery', as he put it. Equiano was beside himself with helpless fury. Things had been looking so good ... and now ... this! Couldn't he trust anyone *at all*?

Doran took him to his own ship, and sailed to the island of Montserrat in the West Indies, selling him on to an American merchant named Robert King, from the Quaker colony of Philadelphia. King was a decent employer, providing his slaves with both a living allowance and better food than many others – but they were still his property. Equiano worked hard in this new position. He'd noticed how other owners on the island treated their slaves much worse, and he didn't want to be sold to any of *them*. He had also seen the punishments dealt out to slaves who offended their owners. One master boasted about once cutting off a slave's leg for 'running away'.

'But you're a Christian!' exclaimed Equiano. 'You go to church on Sundays! How can you answer to God for doing that? Jesus told us to do to others that which we would want done unto us!'

'Maybe,' replied the owner, smiling. 'But it stopped the slave from running away, didn't it? And it warned the others.'

What could you say to that? Equiano continued to work as best as he could, even if it meant being put in charge of other slaves. He wondered whether being a good 'owner' made slavery justifiable – after all, it was normal back in Africa. People in his own village *had* kept slaves, but never treated them as brutally as he saw here, with masters using chains, muzzles, handcuffs, leg-bolts, whips, thumbscrews and other punishments, along with savage beatings and imprisonments. Even worse – it was all legal. Equiano learned that the maximum fine for any owner killing a slave in Barbados was 'fifteen pounds' – not much for a human life. 'Was that all a person was worth?' he wondered.

He heard some owners say that their slaves had to be treated like animals because they were incapable of being anything better, as they came from a place (Africa) where nature had left them 'unfinished'. 'Unfinished?' It was all just a gigantic lie being constantly repeated to justify their cruelty. His own master treated him well, but the other owners dreaded facing a slave revolt – and fear seemed to bring out the worst in them.

The Quakers of Barbados

Robert King, Equiano's owner, was a member of the *Society of Friends*, commonly known as Quakers. This Christian group believed in the equal worth of all, believing that God was 'in every person'. As a result, they opposed elaborate religious ceremony, decorative clothing, the making of war, the taking of oaths, the keeping of titles and even the calling of each other by anything other than 'Brother' or 'Sister'. Founded by George Fox in the mid-1600s, this simple faith was followed by many throughout the English-speaking world – even on slave-owning islands like Barbados. Fox visited the island in 1671, asking his fellow-believers,

> 'Did not Christ die for the Blacks and the Taunies, as well as for the Whites? And was not [Christ's] blood shed for all men, and are they not men?'

It was dangerous talk. One Quaker map-maker was commissioned to create a map of the island for the Governor – and left out the fortresses and watch-towers that were placed to protect against slave revolts! By Olaudah Equiano's time, government pressure had driven many Quakers to seek an easier life in Philadelphia – but a few, like King, remained to do business, believing that slavery was justified if you treated your slaves fairly. Others believed it was utterly wrong, and began to campaign against it. The *Society for the Abolition of the Slave Trade* first met in London in 1787. Most of the original members were Quakers, using their business organisation skills to contribute pamphlets, leaflets, debates and talks on the subject. Their influence on the cause would be immense. Thomas Buxton, a Quaker serving as a Member of the British Parliament, later took the lead in the abolition campaign in the House of Commons when its first leader (William Wilberforce) retired.

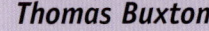

Thomas Buxton

Taunies: a term used in the 18th and 19th centuries to describe people of mixed race (not used today)

What Do You Think?

1. Why do you think Captain Doran threatened to punish Equiano for speaking too much English?

2. Equiano was furious about the way in which Captain Doran treated him but Robert King treated him relatively well. Why do you think Equiano still wasn't content?

3. How did Equiano think that their Christian beliefs should make the slave owners act differently?

4. On what grounds would a Quaker oppose slavery? How might Robert King have justified his decision to carry on owning slaves? Do you think he was right, as a Quaker, to have slaves? Why?/Why not?

5. Some people thought being a 'good owner' made slavery justifiable. What other situations can you think of where some people excuse injustice in a similar way? Are any of the 'excuses' valid?

Freedom!

Despite being enslaved himself, Equiano started doing a little 'buying and selling' of slaves for himself as he travelled, and began building up savings towards the day when he could buy his own freedom, with Robert King's permission. It was difficult – sometimes white men would cheat him in a deal because they saw no need to honour promises made to a 'mere' African. Once, he was even beaten up and left for dead simply because a man didn't like the look of his face. As he recovered, Equiano decided that once free, the best and safest place to live would be 'Old England'. Other free Africans had made it their home already. King remained a good employer, and promised Equiano his freedom for the sum of forty pounds, and sent him on further business trips around the islands and along the American coast. His savings grew.

Then one day in 1766, Equiano realised he had saved enough. King kept his word, and agreed to set him free. Equiano ran down the street to the local Register office, telling everyone he met that today was the day. 'My feet scarcely touched the ground, for they were winged with joy,' he recalled. The registrar congratulated him, let him have his special licence at half-price – and Equiano dashed back to King to have it signed. With the stroke of a pen, it was done. Unbelievable! Afterwards, he tried to sum up his feelings about how 'I, who had been a slave in the morning, trembling at the will of another, now became my own master, and completely free.' Now, he could begin a new life – but he would still have to be careful. Life for a freed slave in the West Indies was sometimes even *more* dangerous than being a slave. Owners would suspect him of giving their own slaves 'ideas', and might try to intimidate him. It had happened to others.

Equiano worked for King for another year, but then decided to leave the islands for good. He made some more business trips, survived a shipwreck, then sailed for London, where he already had friends. Once there, he promptly got himself employed as a personal servant on more voyages around the Atlantic, the Mediterranean and even North as far as the Arctic Circle in search of the 'North-East Passage' – the hoped-for route to India via the North Pole! On that journey he saw whales, walruses and more, and even stepped out across ice-floes to hunt polar bears.

But during these voyages, Equiano made a further discovery – that he was not at peace with himself. There

Black Londoners

Equiano wasn't the first enslaved African to make England his home. London had the beginnings of a sizeable Black population in the 1700s, many of whom had initially been taken from Africa as part of the slave trade.

Ukawsaw Gronniosaw had come to England in 1762 after serving with the British Army in Martinique and Cuba. He had a difficult time and was often cheated by those around him, but a friend helped him to write about his experiences in a book that sold well. He wrote that after one misfortune, 'I could scarcely believe it possible that a place where many eminent Christians had lived and preached could abound with so much wickedness and deceit … I cried like a child!'

Ignatius Sancho did rather better, despite being born on a slave-ship and losing both parents by the age of three. He found employment as a butler to the gentry, opened a grocery shop, and then became attached to London's fashionable society. He made friends with famous men from the literary world such as the diarist Samuel Johnson, the actor David Garrick, and the author Laurence Sterne. A 'man of letters', he wrote in scathing terms about the 'abominable traffic' in slaves – and even had his portrait painted by Thomas Gainsborough.

---

were so many questions, so many bad memories that lurked at the back of his mind – fears for the future, and fears of death. He was curious about the different types of religious faith that existed in the world, and found some comfort in reading passages from the Bible, but he wanted something more than just having rules for living a good life. Something else 'out there' was fascinating him, drawing him further on, but he couldn't quite understand what it was. He started attending informal services in churches and Methodist chapels, and listened hard to the preachers. Then, one night whilst on a voyage to Spain, Equiano had a spiritual experience as he prayed. He pictured Jesus dying on the Cross, bearing all the humiliations and horrors of the world – like a slave. But there was more: this death was also pouring out God's forgiveness for all humanity. Afterwards, Equiano wrote:

'I [now knew] what it was to be born again … Now every providential circumstance that happened to me, from the day I was taken from my parents to that hour, was then, as if it had but just then occurred. I was sensible of the invisible hand of God, which guided me and protected me, when in truth I knew it not … this mercy melted me down.'

It was an astonishing change. The fears of death and destruction that had plagued him for so many years had gone. Equiano had discovered something completely new in his life. He now felt 'entirely at liberty' – completely free.

What Do You Think?

1. What difference did it make to Equiano when he bought his freedom?

2. Equiano found that he was not content although he was at last a free man. Why do you think people can feel a sense of anticlimax after a dream has come true? Are there any times when something like this has happened to you?

3. What difference did it make to Equiano when he experienced God for himself?

Fighting Slavery

Equiano embarked on more business trips for different clients – but then discovered something disturbing. There was a legal case coming up in the courts concerning a slave-ship called the *Zong*, whose slaves had been dumped overboard. The *Zong's* insurers were now challenging the owners' insurance claim. A member of the ship's crew named James Kelsall had decided to give evidence *against* the owners. Equiano bristled as he heard more. An *insurance claim?* Why weren't the ship's owners being charged with *murder?* He contacted Granville Sharp, a government civil servant (and a member of the Clapham Sect) who had been interested in these matters ever since the day he'd had a runaway slave freed in a court case. Sharp agreed to help, and tried to get the *Zong's* owners prosecuted for murder. He failed, but the attempt won a lot of useful publicity for those campaigning against the Trade.

There were now more people speaking out against the Trade. A friend of Equiano's at Oxford University had sponsored an essay competition ('Is it right for human beings to enslave one another?') and one student's winning essay was published. The student, Thomas Clarkson, started researching the subject further, met others of similar opinion – and decided to dedicate his whole life to halting both the Trade and even slavery itself. The *Society for the Abolition of the Slave Trade* was formed in 1787, and Clarkson became its chief researcher in England, collecting information from sailors, merchants and ex-slaves to create the world's first popular human rights campaign. William Wilberforce (MP for Hull, and another Clapham Sect member) was invited to lead the parliamentary campaign; famous people, such as the author Hannah More and Dr James Ramsey (also from the Clapham Sect), the artist Joshua Reynolds, and the potter Josiah Wedgwood, all volunteered their different skills towards creating a change in popular opinion about the rights and wrongs of slavery.

> Modern human rights movements such as 'Make Poverty History' owe a lot of their campaigning ideas to Clarkson's methods. Did you think the Make Poverty History wristband was a modern idea? Josiah Wedgwood was commissioned by Clarkson's group to create a badge containing a simple logo and caption 'Am I not a man and a brother' that was worn as a fashion accessory. Thousands of badges were made, sold and given away.

People Power

The abolition campaign saw a new form of politics taking place across the country, as small local groups began their own campaigns against both the slave trade and slavery itself. These campaigners led meetings, organised boycotts of goods produced by slave labour, produced petitions, put up posters, raised funds, and circulated hundreds of leaflets and booklets to voice their concerns. Many of those involved were Christians, and church buildings were often used for meetings. A great deal of the campaign material used texts from the Bible to hammer its message home about 'all being equal in the sight of God,' who valued everyone, both 'slave and free'.

The *Society for Abolition* co-ordinated the campaign, but Thomas Clarkson also used local contacts to collect further damning evidence of the awful effects of the Trade on the lives of the sailors who went on these voyages. Many sailors had witnessed terrible things happening both to slaves and their fellow crew, and wanted to see justice done. Sometimes Clarkson went in fear of his life, as some slave-ship captains were quite prepared to pay to silence him *permanently*.

The Quaker Elizabeth Heyrick's *Birmingham Ladies' Society for the Relief of Negro Slaves* is one example of a powerful local women's group that formed a network supplying the national campaign with funds. In 1830, she convinced a national conference that the *Anti-Slavery Society* (as it had now become) should stop talking about 'gradual abolition' and instead call for 'immediate abolition'. She won.

Campaign banner from 1830s

Meanwhile, Equiano prepared his own contribution – an autobiography detailing all the abuses he had seen and suffered, his adventures on the high seas, his thoughts on slavery – and his own spiritual journey. He sought out 'lists of subscribers' (supporters willing to pay in advance to finance the publication), and in 1789 produced *The Interesting Narrative of the Life of Olaudah Equiano, or Gustavus Vassa, the African, Written by Himself*. It sold well, requiring nine further editions to meet the demand. Equiano began marketing the book himself, making 'book tours' of the British Isles, giving public talks on his experiences, and joining in popular debates about slavery.

Anti-slavery badge

By 1794, he had earned enough to retire, and did so, like an English gentleman. He had married Susanna Cullen in 1792 and they had two daughters, one of whom survived and inherited £950 (equivalent to £100 000 today), the other died aged four and is buried in Cambridgeshire. The campaign against slavery faltered as Britain faced up to the perils of the French Revolution and Napoleon. Now was not a good time to press the case for slave freedom – but it would come again one day, Equiano knew that. Freedom would come – and he wasn't frightened any more.

Olaudah Equiano died on 31 March 1797. The slave trade was abolished by the British Government in 1807, two years after Nelson's successful sea battle at Trafalgar. The Emancipation Act (setting free all slaves in British colonies) was passed in 1833, and became effective in 1838.

The name Equiano means 'when he speaks they listen' or an orator.

The 1833 Act was known officially as the *Act for the Total Abolition of Colonial Slavery*, but is usually known as the *Slave Emancipation Act*. It was passed in 1833 and came into force in August 1834. It gave all slaves in the British Empire their freedom. In reality enslaved Africans in the colonies were forced to work as 'apprentices' for their ex-masters until 1838.

What Do You Think?

1. The 1807 Act to Abolish the Slave Trade was brought before Parliament as a result of many different people working together. What do you think motivated these people to campaign against slavery? Give as many reasons as you can.

2. How far do you think Equiano's Christian faith influenced his decision to join the campaign?

Biographical Notes

1510	King Ferdinand of Spain gives permission for taking enslaved Africans from Africa to the Americas
c.1745	Olaudah Equiano born
c.1756	Equiano captured aged around 11
1759	Equiano baptised as a Christian
c.1762	Ukawsaw Gronniosaw comes to England
1766	Equiano buys his freedom
1767	Equiano returns to London
c.1770	Ukawsaw Gronniosaw publishes his autobiography
1772	Ottobah Cugoano transported to England and gains his freedom
1780	William Wilberforce enters Parliament as MP for Hull
1781	The *Zong* Massacre
1785	John Newton persuades William Wilberforce to lead the parliamentary campaign against slavery
1787	May: the Society for the Abolition of the Slave Trade first meets
1787	Cugoano publishes his autobiography
c.1788	Mary Prince born in Bermuda
1789	Equiano publishes his autobiography
1792	Start of the Clapham Sect
1792	Resolution for the gradual abolition of the slave trade defeated in the House of Lords
1792	Equiano marries Susanna Cullen
1797	Equiano dies
1804	Wilberforce's Bill passed in the Commons, but rejected in the Lords
1807	25 March: British Parliament passes the Act to Abolish the Slave Trade
1807	21 December: John Newton dies
1808	US abolishes the slave trade
1825	Thomas Fowell Buxton takes over from William Wilberforce as leader of the parliamentary campaign
1828	Mary Prince taken to England
1831	Mary Prince publishes her autobiography
1833	The *Slave Emancipation Act* passed by the British Parliament
1838	The *Slave Emancipation Act* becomes effective
1840	Joseph Turner paints 'Slave Ship'
1865	Slavery abolished in US territories

Things to Do

1 **Either** Think back to the story of the *Zong* massacre and the description of the Deadly Trangle. List the arguments for and against slavery. Think about: how the slave-traders viewed their slaves; the benefits for the slave-traders; the ways in which countries like England benefited from slavery and how ideas about slavery were changed by the Transatlantic Slave Trade.

Or It is 1781: plan and conduct a class debate between those who are pro-slavery and those who are against it.

2 Imagine you are James Kelsall writing your diary on the *Zong*. Note down your feelings and your arguments against the captain's decisions.

3 Use the descriptions of life on a slave-ship written by Equiano, Cugoano and John Newton to help you script a conversation between two slaves about the conditions on the voyage to America.

4 Slavery has existed in various forms throughout history. Read the Bible story of when the Egyptians enslaved the Hebrew people (the Israelites), and their eventual escape, which Jews today celebrate with a Passover meal. You can find this story in Exodus chapters 1–12 in the Bible. What are the parallels between this story of the Israelite slaves in Egypt and events of the Transatlantic Slave Trade as recounted in Equiano's story? In groups, prepare computer presentations for the class about the similarities and differences between the two events.

5 Use a Bible to help you think through what Christians believe about slavery:

(a) 'Slaves' were common in the time of Jesus and the New Testament writers. In many circumstances, these slaves were servants who were well educated, and had very responsible jobs in households. Look up the advice which St Paul gave to slaves and masters in his letter to the Ephesians 6:5–9 in the Bible. How should they behave towards each other? When Paul wrote that, do you think he could have imagined the cruelty and inhumanity of the Transatlantic Slave Trade?

(b) Christians also believe that God created people in his own image and that he views all people as equal. Look this up in the following Bible passages: Genesis 1:26–27, Romans 10:12, Colossians 3:11 and Galatians 3:28.

(c) Jesus also taught his followers to love God and to love their neighbour as themselves (you can find this in Matthew 22:34–40). Work out what it would really mean if you were to love your neighbour as yourself.

Consider what you have learned from these Bible passages. If you were Paul writing instructions to Christian slaves and masters about how to behave towards each other, what would you say?

6 Many people involved in the Transatlantic Slave Trade were Christians. Why do you think it took so long before Christians spoke out against slavery? What blinded them to the issues?

In groups, identify and discuss issues to which people seem blind today. What blindfolds them? Create a group mime to demonstrate one issue: think about how to portray the issue and how to represent the things that make people turn a blind eye.

7 Either Imagine you are an Abolitionist living in the 1790s. Write an article for a Christian publication to wake people up to the issues.

Or Choose a contemporary issue that you believe is wrong, but to which many Christians seem to turn a blind eye. Write an article to put onto a Christian website to convince Christians that they need to take action on this issue.

8 Christians are often baptised to show that they believe in Jesus. Equiano was baptised in 1759 as part of his efforts to 'improve himself out of slavery'. Attending church taught him a lot about Jesus and about what Christians believe. Several years later, Equiano describes having a spiritual experience of being 'born again' as he prayed while on a voyage to Spain. Compare Equiano's experience with that of an early disciple of Jesus called Saul, on the road to Damascus as recorded in the Bible in Acts 9:1–18. Draw a timeline showing key points in Equiano's faith journey as a Christian, with explanatory notes about what happened.

9 Imagine that a major blockbuster about William Wilberforce is to be filmed. It will be about his life, his Christian beliefs and values, and his fight to abolish the slave trade. Research Wilberforce's life. Draw an annotated storyboard for the film showing the key events from his life and the campaign that you would want to include.

10 Equiano worked hard to earn money to buy his freedom. This included buying and selling slaves. Why do you think he did this? Later, when he was campaigning against slavery, how might he have explained what he had done? Write a speech that Equiano might have made to justify this.

11 Equiano's name means 'when he speaks, they listen'. Christians believe that God gives gifts to people to use for the good of others. List Equiano's gifts. Explain how Equiano used his God-given gifts. In groups, list each other's gifts and discuss ways of using your gifts to help others.

12
> Amazing grace, how sweet the sound
> That saved a wretch like me,
> I once was lost, but now am found,
> Was blind, but now I see.
> 'Twas grace that taught my heart to fear,
> And grace my fears relieved.
>
> How precious did that grace appear
> The hour I first believed.
> Through many dangers, toils and snares,
> I have already come.
> 'Tis grace hath brought me safe thus far,
> And grace will lead me home.

John Newton was the writer of the well-known Christian hymn 'Amazing Grace'. Find out more about his life. Then try to work out what he might have meant by these words and phrases in the hymn: wretch; lost; found; blind; dangers, toils and snares.

The word 'grace' in this hymn means 'a free, unearned or undeserved favour or gift from God'. Explain to a partner what John Newton might have meant that God had given him, or done for him, which he did not deserve, and why he described that as 'amazing'. As a class, create an 'Amazing Grace' wall chart. Put 'Amazing Grace' at the centre, with the words of the hymn underneath. Then write on it all the things that John Newton might have meant by that phrase.

13 What role did Churches play in slavery and the abolition campaign? Why were some Christians particularly concerned to campaign against slavery? Make a list of modern-day campaigns against injustice where you can find that Christians have played a part.

14 On 8 February 2006, the Church of England's parliament, the General Synod, issued an apology for the Church's involvement in the Transatlantic Slave Trade, as slavers, as plantation owners and as those who profited from the Trade. Archbishop Rowan Williams said, 'To speak here of repentance and apology is not words alone; it is part of our witness to the Gospel, to a world that needs to hear that the past must be faced and healed and cannot be ignored.' Discuss what the Archbishop meant by his words. In 2 groups, prepare speeches that could have been made in the General Synod debate, for and against the Church apologising for the slave trade.

Religious and Moral Education Press
A division of SCM-Canterbury Press Ltd
A wholly owned subsidiary of
Hymns Ancient & Modern Ltd
St Mary's Works, St Mary's Plain
Norwich, Norfolk NR3 3BH

Story copyright © 2007 Christopher K. Hudson

Questions copyright © 2007 The Stapleford Centre

Christopher K. Hudson has asserted his right under the Copyright, Designs and Patents Act, 1988 to be identified as Author of this Work.

All rights reserved. No part of this publication may be reproduced, stored in a retrieval system, or transmitted, in any form or by any means, electronic, electrostatic, magnetic tape, mechanical, photocopying, recording or otherwise, without permission in writing from the publishers.

First published 2007

ISBN 978 1 85175 341 3

Designed and typeset by
TOPICS – The Creative Partnership, Exeter

Printed in Great Britain by Brightsea Press, Exeter for SCM-Canterbury Press Ltd, Norwich

Notes for Teachers

The first *Faith in Action* books were published in the late 1970s and the series has remained popular with both teachers and pupils. However, much in education has changed over the last twenty years, such as the development of both new examination syllabuses in Religious Studies and local agreed syllabuses for Religious Education which place more emphasis on pupils' own understanding, interpretation and evaluation of religious belief and practice, rather than a simple knowledge of events. This has encouraged us to amend the style of the *Faith in Action* Series to make it more suitable for today's classroom.

The aim is, as before, to tell the stories of people who have lived and acted according to their faith, but we have included alongside the main story questions which will encourage pupils to think about the reasons for the behaviour of our main characters and to empathise with the situations in which they found themselves. We hope that pupils will also be able to relate some of the issues in the stories to other issues in modern society, either in their own area or on a global scale.

The 'What Do You Think?' questions may be used for group or class discussion or for short written exercises. The 'Things to Do' at the end of the story include ideas for longer activities for RE or Citizenship and offer opportunities for assessment.

In line with current syllabus requirements, as Britain is a multifaith society, Faith in Action characters are selected from a variety of faith backgrounds and many of the questions may be answered from the perspective of more than one faith.

Acknowledgements

This is one of three *Faith in Action* books and a Teacher's Resource on CD-ROM published in association with **set all free** ACT TO END SLAVERY, a project of Churches Together in England to commemorate the bicentenary in 2007 of the Act to Abolish the Slave Trade. Further information can be found at www.setallfree.net

These publications have been developed by the **set all free** education group, consisting of Uzoamaka Agyare-Kumi, Linda Ali, Alison Farnell, Sarah Lane, Tessa Oram, Richard Reddie, Sally Smith and Kate Yates, who have all made significant contributions to the content.

Staff at The Stapleford Centre have helped to produce this series – www.stapleford-centre.org

Anti-Slavery International has given invaluable help in providing images to be used in this publication – www.antislavery.org